Take Your Pick!

# TAKE YOUR PICK OF

# HAUNTED PLACES

BY G.G. LAKE

Raintree is an imprint of Capstone Global Library Limited, a company incorporated in England and Wales having its registered office at 264 Banbury Road, Oxford, OX2 7DY – Registered company number: 6695582

www.raintree.co.uk
myorders@raintree.co.uk

Edited by Nikki Potts
Designed by Kyle Grenz
Picture research by Tracey Engel
Production by Kathy McColley
Originated by Capstone Global Library Ltd
Printed and bound in China.

ISBN 978 1 4747 3593 3
20 19 18 17 16
10 9 8 7 6 5 4 3 2 1

**British Library Cataloguing in Publication Data**
A full catalogue record for this book is available from the British Library.

**Acknowledgements**
We would like to thank the following for permission to reproduce photographs:
Alamy: David Wall, 20, The Marsden Archive, 7; AP Photo: Dylan Lovan, 8; iStockphoto: Dieter Spears, 5; Matthew Bordignon, 27; Shutterstock: Alexander Chaikin, 17, CREATISTA, 11, Everett Historical, 15, Freedom Man, back cover and spine, Gordon Bell, 16, iolya, 24, Jacqueline Abromeit, front cover (top), Jakub.it, 9, Karen Grigoryan, 13, MarcAndreLeTourneux, 12, Songquan Deng, front cover (bottom); Superstock: Design Pics, 22; The Image Works: FrithMary Evans, 6; Wikimedia: Cobra97/CC-BY-SA-3.0, 25, Constantin Barbu/CC BY 2.0, 18, Felix O/CC-BY-SA-2.0, 23, Nancy/ CC-BY-SA-4.0,3.0,2.5,2.0,1.0, 10, Pugin and Rowlandson, 1808/CC-PD-Mark, 21, Reading Tom/CC-BY-2.0, 19, Shadowgate/CC BY 2.0, 14, Tim Kiser/CC-BY-SA-2.5, 26

Every effort has been made to contact copyright holders of material reproduced in this book. Any omissions will be rectified in subsequent printings if notice is given to the publisher.

All the internet addresses (URLs) given in this book were valid at the time of going to press. However, due to the dynamic nature of the internet, some addresses may have changed, or sites may have changed or ceased to exist since publication. While the author and publisher regret any inconvenience this may cause readers, no responsibility for any such changes can be accepted by either the author or the publisher.

# CONTENTS

# GHOST HUNT

Imagine you are a ghost hunter. You're ready for the hunt. In your pack are a torch, a mobile phone and a camera. If there's a ghost, you'll find it. There are so many places said to be **haunted** in the world. Take your pick!

**haunted**  having mysterious events happen often, possibly due to visits from ghosts

# ATHELHAMPTON HOUSE
## OR BORLEY RECTORY

**Would you pick Athelhampton House or Borley Rectory?**

## ATHELHAMPTON HOUSE

### LOCATION: DORSET, ENGLAND

▶ Two ghosts fight with swords in the Great Hall.

▶ The Grey Lady haunts the east end of the building. A maid once saw this ghost walk through a wall.

▶ The ghost of a pet ape scratches the inside of the walls.

# BORLEY RECTORY

## LOCATION: ESSEX, ENGLAND

### BACKGROUND: THE RECTORY BURNED DOWN IN 1939. TODAY GHOST HUNTERS STILL VISIT THE SITE.

► A nun's ghost walks the gardens looking for her lost love.

► In the 1930s a couple said a mean ghost attacked them. It broke windows and threw bottles.

► People **reported** seeing a ghostly **carriage** pulled by horses go through the gates.

**report** written or spoken account of something that has happened

**carriage** vehicle with wheels that is usually pulled by horses

# WAVERLY HILLS SANATORIUM OR ALCATRAZ ISLAND

Would you pick Waverly Hills Sanatorium or Alcatraz Island?

## WAVERLY HILLS SANATORIUM

### LOCATION: LOUISVILLE, KENTUCKY, USA

► A ghost named Timmy is said to live there. Timmy likes to roll balls back and forth with visitors.

► A ghostly old woman runs from the building. People have heard her scream "Help me!" and "Somebody save me!"

► During the 1900s workers got rid of dead bodies using a tunnel. Today voices and footsteps can be heard in the tunnel.

# ALCATRAZ ISLAND

## LOCATION: NEAR SAN FRANCISCO BAY, USA
## BACKGROUND: THE US GOVERNMENT RAN A PRISON ON THE ISLAND FROM 1934 TO 1963.

▶ People have reported unexplained moaning, weird smells and cold spots at the prison.

▶ Many workers have reported hearing banjo music play softly from the prison showers.

▶ According to American Indian **legends**, evil ghosts haunt the island.

**legend** story handed down from earlier times; legends are often based on fact, but they are not entirely true

# WOODCHESTER MANSION
## OR WINCHESTER MYSTERY HOUSE

**Would you pick Woodchester Mansion or Winchester Mystery House?**

WOODCHESTER MANSION

## LOCATION: GLOUCESTER, ENGLAND

► A worker's dog is said to see the **mansion's** ghosts and lick their hands.

► A floating head scares visitors in the women's bathroom.

► The ghost of an old woman sometimes attacks young female visitors.

**mansion** very large house

# WINCHESTER MYSTERY HOUSE

## LOCATION: SAN JOSE, CALIFORNIA, USA

► The 160-room house was designed oddly. Stairs lead to nowhere, and doors open to walls.

► Sarah Winchester, the past owner, haunts the room where she died.

► Visitors feel cold spots and hear voices of past servants.

# EDINBURGH CASTLE
## OR THE WHITE HOUSE

**Would you pick Edinburgh Castle or the White House?**

## EDINBURGH CASTLE

### LOCATION: EDINBURGH, SCOTLAND

▶ The ghost of a young boy bangs on a drum. It is said he only appears before an attack on the castle.

▶ Visitors to the castle say they have felt tugs on their clothing. They've also seen strange shadows.

▶ A friendly ghost dog haunts the castle's **cemetery**.

**cemetery**  place where dead people are buried

# THE WHITE HOUSE

## LOCATION: WASHINGTON DC, USA

▶ The ghost of former US president Abraham Lincoln haunts many rooms of the White House.

▶ The ghost of former US president Andrew Jackson haunts the Rose Room.

▶ The ghost of past First Lady Abigail Adams has been seen hanging laundry in the East Room.

# CULLODEN MOOR
## OR GETTYSBURG

**Would you pick Culloden Moor or Gettysburg?**

## CULLODEN MOOR

**LOCATION: SCOTLAND, UNITED KINGDOM**

**BACKGROUND: A BLOODY BATTLE BETWEEN BRITISH AND SCOTTISH SOLDIERS TOOK PLACE HERE ON 16 APRIL, 1746.**

▶ Ghosts of dead soldiers haunt Culloden Moor. It is said the ghosts are most active on April 16th.

▶ Visitors can hear shouts and swords banging.

▶ A ghost of a Scottish soldier walks around saying "**defeated**" softly.

**defeat** beat someone in a war, fight or competition

# GETTYSBURG

## LOCATION: PENNSYLVANIA, USA

### BACKGROUND: ONE OF THE BLOODIEST BATTLES IN THE US CIVIL WAR (1861–1865) TOOK PLACE HERE.

► Present-day photos of Little Round Top hill show **orbs**.

► Ghost soldiers line up as if they are about to fight.

► In the Gettysburg College basement, ghostly doctors from the war help hurt ghost soldiers.

**orb** glowing ball of light that sometimes appears in photographs taken at reportedly haunted locations; many people believe orbs are signs of ghosts

# HAMPTON COURT PALACE
## OR THE TOWER OF LONDON

**Would you pick Hampton Court Palace or the Tower of London?**

## HAMPTON COURT PALACE

### LOCATION: LONDON, ENGLAND

▶ Past queen Catherine Howard haunts the palace **gallery**.

▶ The ghost of Sybil Penn, servant to four previous monarchs, haunts the state apartments and Clock Court.

▶ In 2003 what looked like a skeleton wearing a **cloak** appeared by a set of doors. It quickly disappeared.

**gallery**  place where art is shown

**cloak**  loose piece of clothing that is used like a coat or cape

# THE TOWER OF LONDON

## LOCATION: LONDON, ENGLAND

### BACKGROUND: ENGLAND HAS USED THE TOWER AS A PALACE AND A PRISON.

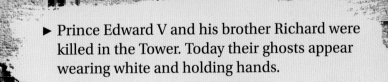

▶ Prince Edward V and his brother Richard were killed in the Tower. Today their ghosts appear wearing white and holding hands.

▶ Anne Boleyn's ghost has been seen running through the courtyard. The past queen was killed at the Tower.

▶ Visitors have reported feeling their throats being crushed.

# IULIA HASDEU CASTLE OR LALAURIE HOUSE

**Would you pick Iulia Hasdeu Castle or LaLaurie House?**

## IULIA HASDEU CASTLE

**LOCATION: CAMPINA, ROMANIA**

**BACKGROUND: BOGDAN PETRICEICU HASDEU BUILT THE CASTLE FOR THE GHOST OF HIS DAUGHTER, IULIA.**

► Hasdeu said he talked with Iulia's ghost in one of the rooms.

► Strange symbols appear on the walls. It's said the symbols help the living connect with the dead.

► Visitors have seen Iulia's ghost playing the piano.

# LALAURIE HOUSE

## LOCATION: NEW ORLEANS, LOUISIANA, USA
## BACKGROUND: MADAME LALAURIE TORTURED ENSLAVED AFRICAN-AMERICANS IN THE HOUSE.

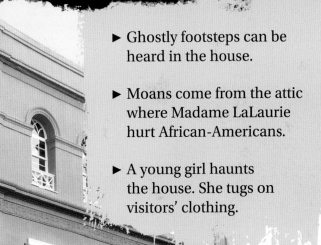

▶ Ghostly footsteps can be heard in the house.

▶ Moans come from the attic where Madame LaLaurie hurt African-Americans.

▶ A young girl haunts the house. She tugs on visitors' clothing.

**torture**  cause someone extreme pain or mental suffering

# EMPRESS THEATRE OR THE THEATRE ROYAL DRURY LANE

**Would you pick the Empress Theatre or the Theatre Royal Drury Lane?**

## EMPRESS THEATRE

### LOCATION: FORT MACLEOD, ALBERTA, CANADA

► A janitor named Ed haunts the Empress Theatre. He sometimes sits and watches plays.

► A man's face appears in bathroom mirrors.

► An actor once reported that a ghost trapped him in the basement.

# THE THEATRE ROYAL DRURY LANE

## LOCATION: LONDON, ENGLAND

▶ Many people have reported seeing a floating white head.

▶ Some people have reported being kicked in the rear by a ghostly clown.

▶ The ghost of a young man wearing a white wig and a grey cloak appears. He is called the Man in Grey.

# HIGHWAY 666 OR
## PLUCKLEY VILLAGE

**Would you pick Highway 666
or Pluckley Village?**

## HIGHWAY 666

### LOCATION: SOUTHWEST UNITED STATES

- ► The ghost of a young girl appears on the side of the highway. She disappears when drivers try to help her.

- ► Evil ghosts are said to try to cause car crashes.

- ► A ghost truck haunts the highway. It's on fire as it speeds down the road.

NORTH
666

NORTH
666

▶ People say there are at least 12 ghosts in the town of Kent.

▶ The ghost of an old woman sits at a bridge. She has been seen smoking a pipe.

▶ A young, beautiful ghost haunts St. Nicholas's Church. She is called the White Lady.

23

# HIGHGATE CEMETERY
## OR BACHELOR'S GROVE CEMETERY

**Would you pick Highgate or Bachelor's Grove Cemetery?**

## HIGHGATE CEMETERY

### LOCATION: LONDON, ENGLAND

- ► Lack of care after World War II (1939-1945) has left the eerie cemetery in disrepair.

- ► A ghost of an old woman screams for her lost children. She runs between **tombstones** looking for them.

- ► A man reported seeing a creature with glowing red eyes.

**tombstone** carved block of stone that marks the place where someone is buried

# BACHELOR'S GROVE CEMETERY

## LOCATION: NEAR CHICAGO, ILLINOIS, USA

▶ A ghost carrying her baby haunts the cemetery. She appears during full moons.

▶ Visitors sometimes see a ghostly house.

▶ A ghostly farmer, horse and plough haunt a nearby pond.

# TRANS-ALLEGHENY LUNATIC ASYLUM
## OR BEECHWORTH LUNATIC ASYLUM

**Would you pick Trans-Allegheny Lunatic Asylum or Beechworth Lunatic Asylum?**

## TRANS-ALLEGHENY LUNATIC ASYLUM

### LOCATION: WESTON, WEST VIRGINIA, USA

- ▶ A ghost named Ruth haunts the first floor. She pushes people who say her name.

- ▶ People have seen doors closing on their own in the **asylum**.

- ▶ The fourth floor is said to be the most haunted. People have heard unexplained voices and banging sounds there.

26     **asylum** hospital for people who are mentally ill

# BEECHWORTH LUNATIC ASYLUM

## LOCATION: BEECHWORTH, VICTORIA, AUSTRALIA

► Visitors have heard ghostly screams and laughter.

► Matron Sharp is the asylum's friendly ghost. She wears a grey hood.

► An old ghost in a green jacket haunts the gardens.

# RAPID ROUND

Which would you pick to play hide and seek in?

THE TOWER OF LONDON OR HIGHGATE CEMETERY?

Which would you go to for a holiday?

WINCHESTER MYSTERY HOUSE OR PLUCKLEY VILLAGE?

Which would you live in with your family?

ATHELHAMPTON HOUSE OR LALAURIE HOUSE?

Where would you film a scary movie?

HIGHWAY 666 OR IULIA HASDEU CASTLE?

Which would you pick to clean?

THE WHITE HOUSE OR THE WINCHESTER HOUSE?

# Which ghost would you like to meet?

## THE WHITE LADY IN PLUCKLEY OR THE MAN IN GRAY IN DRURY LANE?

# Which ghost pet would you pick?

## A DOG OR AN APE?

# Which would you pick for a picnic?

## GETTYSBURG OR BACHELOR'S GROVE CEMETERY?

# Which would you pick for a sleepover with friends?

## TRANS-ALLEGHENY LUNATIC ASYLUM OR EMPRESS THEATRE?

# Which would you rather hear?

## GHOSTLY LAUGHTER OR GHOSTLY FOOTSTEPS?

# GLOSSARY

**asylum** hospital for people who are mentally ill

**carriage** vehicle with wheels that is usually pulled by horses

**cemetery** place where dead people are buried

**cloak** loose piece of clothing that is used like a coat or cape

**defeat** beat someone in a war, fight or competition

**gallery** place where art is shown

**legend** story handed down from earlier times; legends are often based on fact, but they are not entirely true

**mansion** very large house

**orb** glowing ball of light that sometimes appears in photographs taken at reportedly haunted locations; many people believe orbs are signs of ghosts

**report** written or spoken account of something that has happened

**tombstone** carved block of stone that marks the place where someone is buried

**torture** cause someone extreme pain or mental suffering

# READ MORE

*Ghosts & Hauntings* (Solving Mysteries with Science), Jane Bingham (Raintree, 2013)

*Ghost Hunting* (Xtreme Adventure), S.L. Hamilton (Franklin Watts, 2015)

*Tracking Ghosts* (Spooked), Emily Raij (Raintree, 2015)

# WEBSITES

**www.haunted-britain.com/**
Check out some of the most haunted places in the United Kingdom and Ireland.

**www.simplyghostnights.co.uk/venues/**
This website has a data base full of haunted places throughout the United Kingdom.